VEGAN RECIPES

ARE MEDICINE

PLANT FOOD FOR YOUR CELLS
THAT FEED & BUILD YOUR
SACRED GEOMETRIC BIOLOGICAL
STRUCTURE

THE
SCAFFOLDING OF LIFE

BY
LOVELIFELEE

PAGE INDEX AT BACK OF BOOK

Published in 2020 by FeedARead.com Publishing

A CIP catalogue record for this title is available from the British Library.

POEMS OF MAGICAL WONDER

POEMS MAGICAL IN NATURE

POEMS OF SPLENDOUR

FROM THE MINDS EYE & HEART SPACE

OF LOVE LIFE LEE

SOME OF MY MAGICAL LIFE JOURNEY

EXPERIENCES OF SHAMANIC CEREMONY

AYAHUASCA CEREMONY'S

PLANT MEDICINE , DREAMS , MEDITATIONS

REMOTE VIEWING , OUT OF BODY JOURNEY'S

AND LIFE EXPERIENCE'S

POEMS AND TRUTHS
OF OUR HOLOGRAPHIC UNIVERSE

THE PHOTON THE LIGHT PARTICLE
IN WHICH WE EXIST AND RESIDE UNTILL
WE EXPAND WITH LIGHT BRIGHTENING
SHINING BRIGHT IN OUR BODYS OF LIGHT

ILLUMINATED OUR RAINBOW BODY's FREE
ANGELS WE BE IMMORTAL
INTERDIMENSIONAL
LIGHT BEINGS OF CONSCIOUS ENERGY

BY LOVE LIFE LEE

LOVE LIFE LEE
YO RASTA !
LOVE LIFE LEE
LIFE LIFE TO THE FULL
FOR ETERNITY
CHANTING AND DANCING
IS WHAT YOU DO BEST
MEDITATION WITH THE SPIRIT'S
YOU TRULY BLESSED
HEAD FULL OF KNOWLEDGE
HEART OF GOLD
WHEN THE GODS MADE YOU
THEY HAD TO BREAK THE MOULD
COS LETS FACE IT DUDE
AND WE ALL AGREE
THIS WORLD CAN ONLY HANDLE
ONE LOVE LIFE LEE

FRONT COVER

THROUGH THESE POEMS MESSAGES OF
ANCIENT KNOWLEDGE & WISDOM ABOUT
ACCESSING YOUR FULLEST POTENTIAL AS A
HUMAN BEING.

LEARNING TO ACCESS YOUR DNA THROUGH

DISCIPLINES PRACTICES MEDITATION YOGA
SHAMANIC CEREMONIES PLANT MEDICINES
ASTRAL TRAVEL DREAMS SPIRIT WORLD
DIET PART OF THE KEY.

EVOLVE CONSCIOUSLY GROW A BODY OF
LIGHT FROM THE BLUE PRINT IN YOUR DNA
TRANSCEND TIME & SPACE.

TRANSVERSE THE UNIVERSE TRAVEL THE
HYPER-DIMENSIONAL MATRIX IN YOUR
RAINBOW ODY OF LIGHT.

YOU ARE AN ETERNAL IMMORTAL
INTERDIMENSIONAL LIGHT BEING OF ULTRA
VIOLET CONSCIOUS ENERGY.

ANGELIC DIVINE INFINITE YOU BE IN AN
OCEAN OF LIGHT IN THE ONENESS OF THE
WHOLE CREATION.

BACK COVER

4

OTHER BOOKS BY LOVELIFELEE

**THE SCAFFOLDING OF LIFE
THE WONDERFUL WORLD OF
GEOMETRIC MATTER
THE BUILDING BLOCKS
OF ALL BIOLOGICAL LIFE &
OUR UNIVERSE
ACCESS THE BLUE PRINT IN
YOUR DNA
GROW A RAINBOW LIGHT BODY
STOP KARMIC CYCLES & EVOLVE
TRANSCEND TIME & SPACE
ASCENSION YOU WILL ACHIEVE
BY LOVE LIFE LEE**

THE SCAFFOLDING OF LIFE
THE BUILDING BLOCKS OF SACRED GEOMETRY
LEARN THE SECRETS OF OUR PHYSICAL UNIVERSE
AND BIOLOGICAL MAKE UP OF OUR DNA, HOW TO
EVOLVE CONSCIOUSLY TRANSCEND TIME & SPACE
TO LEARN HOW TO TRANSVERSE THE
UNIVERSE WITH THOUGHT MIND BODY & SPIRIT
USING YOUR CONSCIOUS ENERGY
USING YOUR LIFE FORCE
UNDERSTAND YOUR FULL POTENTIAL GROW
A NEW BODY INTO BEING CONSCIOUSLY EVOLVE
AND ASCEND CREATE A RAINBOW BODY OF
LIGHT YOUR DIVINE RIGHT

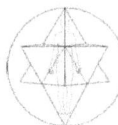

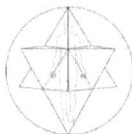

FRONT COVER

5

WISDOM OF MAGICAL WONDER

WISDOM MAGICAL IN NATURE

WISDOM OF SPLENDOUR

FROM THE MINDS EYE & HEART SPACE

OF LOVE LIFE LEE

THROUGH THIS BOOK MESSAGES OF ANCIENT
KNOWLEDGE AND WISDOM ABOUT ACCESSING
YOUR FULLEST POTENTIAL AS A HUMAN BEING
LEARNING TO ACCESS YOUR DNA THROUGH
DISCIPLINE'S PRACTICE'S MEDITATION YOGA
SHAMANIC CEREMONIES PLANT MEDICINES
AYAHUASCA CEREMONIES ASTAL TRAVEL
DREAMS SPIRIT WORLD DIET PART OF THE KEY
AND EVOLVE CONSCIOUSLY GROW A BODY OF LIGHT
FROM THE BLUE PRINT IN YOUR DNA
TRANSCEND TIME AND SPACE
TRANSVERSE THE UNIVERSE TRAVEL THE
HYPER-DIMENSIONAL MATRIX IN YOUR RAINBOW
BODY OF LIGHT
YOU ARE AN IMMORTAL INTERDIMENSIONAL LIGHT
BEING OF ULTRA VIOLET CONSCIOUSNESS ENERGY
ANGELIC DIVINE INFINITE YOU BE
IN AN OCEAN OF LIGHT IN THE ONENESS OF THE
WHOLE CREATION

Spiritual knowledge of the journey
Within and without gaining the understanding
of the scaffolding of life the building blocks of the magical
world of geometric matter the dodecahedrons & tetrahedrons
and life force energy of our selfs and our universe understand
frequencies light vibration in sacred geometry it's wisdom
connecting to the stars
Connecting to nature
Connecting to Energy fields
An awakening , the shaman and i am
A spirit being
An Immortal Interdimensional Light Being
OF Conscious Energy
Divine we be you and me by Divine Decree
Namaste
Blessings to all that be in the oneness of all the creation

BACK COVER

6

INTRODUCTION

PLANT FOOD FUEL FOR THE CELLS

This vegan recipe book has many recipes from plants, plants are medicine for the Avatar the human biological body sytem, your body is built by the way of THE SCAFFOLDING OF LIFE via the building blocks of geometric matter, down past the level of the cells, that we nourish with nutrients, at the micron levels of the cells is the sacred geometry shapes, that are the building blocks of your body, your cells are built with DODECAHEDRONS, and the corners on the Dodecahedron are the only solid mass, the corners relate to amino acids in food, they the amino acids feed the corners of the dodecahedron. Then we come the TETRAHEDRONS which can spin in a hundred and twenty different patterns to create a hundred and twenty different types of protein, and the tetrahedron is spinning inside the dodecahedron.

So it so important we see plants not just as food but as medicine, its quite remarkable that you can ingest a particular raw herb plant, and it will go to thirty eight different parts of the body to feed and heal the building blocks of sacred geometric form, in general we should have a diet of high vibrational plant foods, this raises our consciousness because the body has the right fuel thats light and also gentle on the body to digest and to build the building blocks of life, on a continuum through out your life, the most important biological technology in this universe is the (avatar) the human biological body.

So there are recipes for starters, main courses, desserts, smoothies, and other vegan foods that are medicine to the body healing the cells and rebuilding your scaffolding of life, via the building blocks of sacred geometric matter, on a continuum regenerating your avatar cells twenty four hours a day, every day of your life, its magical, for sentient eternal inter-dimensional light beings we be, your DNA flashing light a hundred HERZ a second, so your DNA flashing light a hundred times every second, you are divine in your light being holographical form, so the right plants, nuts, leaves, barks, saps, roots, flowers, herbs, vegetables, fruits are vital for general heath and well being and also for prevention of disease in the body, so here are dishes to feast on full of flavour, tantalizingly tickling those taste buds as the flavours burst fourth, the senses are on over load the tastes and the aromas, wish you well on your vegan diet and using plant foods as medicines and prevention of disease in the body.

Within our DNA is the schematic for a light body it is the blue print for your eternal immortal body of light, for the truth be know we are eternal interdimensional light beings of divine ultra violet energetic consciousness, manifested in these human avatars for an experience and to grow spiritually, with a vegan plant based diet and ancient practices like meditation, yoga and martial arts for our energy chi flow systems the meridian and chakra systems, and or healing energy practices and shamanic fire ceremonies, we ca raise our bodies vibration and our consciousness and access our light bodies, then being fully embodied but able to travel in the stars in the hyper-dimensional matrix the cosmos, diet is key.

SIMPLE

VEGAN RECIPES

FOR BEGINNERS

Vegan food is easy to make, but these simple 100 vegan recipes will fuel your avatar your biological body allowing it to run at a higher optimal level, some can be prepared less than hour, these delicious recipes range from a wide range of delicious nutritious starters and mains to healthy smoothies and a nice selection of desserts . So if you're looking to add healthier nutritious food and more plants into your diet, or have family and friends that are vegaterian or vegan, then give these recipes a try and serve a vegan dinner to your guests, these simple vegan recipes will go down a treat.

50

SMOOTHIES

QUICK AND EASY
HEALTHY
FULL OF PURE
NUTRITIONAL ENERGY

THAT WILL FEED, FUEL AND HEAL
THE CORNERS OF YOUR SACRED
GEOMETRIC BUILDING BLOCK
STRUCTURES THE
DODECAHEDRONS AND
TETRAHEDRONS THAT BUILD THE
SCAFFOLDING OF LIFE, THE
AVATAR, THE BIOLOGICAL
SYSTEM, THE MOST IMPORTANT
TECHNOLOGY IN THIS UNIVERSE.

SO WE MUST CHANGE OUR
PERSPECTIVE ON FOOD AND OUR

INTAKE OF IT, WE MUST START TO SEE IT AS MEDICINE AND UNDERSTAND THE DEEPEST LEVELS OF HOW THE HUMAN BIOLOGICAL BODY IS ON A CONSTANT CONTINUUM OF REGENERATION, AND THAT WE ARE LIGHT BEINGS VIBRATING AT A FREQUENCY, A DENSITY OF LIGHT, FOR OUR DNA IS FLASHING A HUNDRED HERZ A SECOND MEANING OUR DNA FLASHES A 100 TIMES A SECOND, SO THE AVATAR THE BIOLOGICAL BODY SYSTEM NEEDS THE RIGHT FOOD FUELS.

SO RAW FOOD LIKE IN SMOOTHIES MEANS THERE IS MORE LIGHT IN THE FOOD PRODUCE, FROM WHEN IT WAS GROWING BY PHOTOSYNTHESIS BY THE SUN LIGHT, SOAKING UP THAT COSMIC LIGHT ENERGY.

WHEN WE COOK FOOD WE COOK
THE LIGHT OUT OF THE PRODUCE,
AN EXAMPLE IS A CABBAGE WHEN
YOU LOOK UNDER A MICROSCOPE
AT IT, AND ITS FULL OF LIGHT
AND AFTER YOU COOK IT AOUND
70% OF THE LIGHT HAS BEEN
COOKED OUT OF IT, SO RAW FOOD
DIET WILL EVENTUALLY WITH
OTHER PRACTICES LIKE
MEDITATION AND ENERGY ARTS
WILL ALLOW YOU TO ACCESS
YOUR ETERNAL LIGHT BODY.

THEN YOU WILL BE FULLY
EMBODIED LIVING ON A 4th/5th
DIMENSIONAL PLANET, BUT ABLE
TO TRAVEL IN THE STARS IN THE
HYPER-DIMENSIONAL MATRIX,
THE ENTIRE COSMOS, EVEN
OUTSIDE TIME AND SPACE IN THE
ETERNAL REALM, WHERE THE
KINGDOM OF LIGHT RESIDES, WE

WILL BE ABLE TO ASCEND AND
TRANSCEND, FOR ANGELS WE BE
DO YOU SEE.

GREEN TEA MANGOED

INGREDIENTS

1 cup cos lettuce
1 cup baby spinach
1 banana
1 ripe mango
1 ½ cups pineapple
1 cup green brewed tea
1 cup distilled ice

APRICOT KALED

INGREDIENTS

1 cup kale
1 big banana
2 apples
6 apricots
1 cup distilled water
1 cup distilled ice
1/8th tsp organic vanillia powder

RAISIN VIBRATIONS

INGREDIENTS

1 banana
½ cup raisins
1 tablespoon chia seed
1/8th tsp nutmeg
2 cups rapini
1 cup distilled water
1 cup distilled ice

MANGO MINT MADNESS

INGREDIENTS

2 mangos
1 cup cos lettuce
1 cup ripe pineapple
1 light handful of fresh mint
1 cup coconut water
1 cup distilled ice

FEELING BERRY GINGER

INGREDIENTS

1 cup black berries
½ cup strawberries
1 cup rasberries
2 cup cos lettuce
1 tsp fresh grated ginger
1 cup distilled water
1 cup distilled ice

MELON THE COCONUT

INGREDIENTS

1 cup baby spinach
2 cups honeydew melon
1 cup coconut water
½ cup coconut milk
1/2 cup distilled ice

PAPAYA PAPAYA MANGO

INGREDIENTS

1 cup mango
1 cup pinapple
1 ½ cup papaya
2 cups baby spinach
1 cup unsweetened almond milk
1 cup distilled ice

HELEN MELON

INGREDIENTS

1 cup honeydew melon
1 cup cantaloupe melon
1 cup lettuce
½ cup watercress
1 tablespoon chia seeds
1 cup distilled water
1 cup distilled ice

PEARING AT THE CUCUMBER

INGREDIENTS

1 medium cucumber
1 ½ pears
1 apple
1 cup turnip greens
4 stalks celery
½ cup vanillia milk
1 cup distilled water
1 cup distilled ice

DRAGON FRUIT MADNESS

INGREDIENTS

2 ½ dragon fruits
1 cup green grapes
2 bananas
2 lychee
1 cup spring mixed green leaves
1 cup distilled water
1 cup distilled ice

DATES ON

INGREDIENTS

½ cup dates
1/8 cup prunes
1 cup romaine lettuce
¼ cup beets leaves
1 cup coconut milk
1 cup distilled ice

KIWIED THE BROCCOLI

INGREDIENTS

1 cup broccoli
1 green crisp apple
½ cup green grapes
½ cup red grapes
3 kiwi fruits
¼ tsp spirulina
1 cup unsweetened almond milk
1 cup distilled ice

TROPICAL PINEAPPLE COCONUT

INGREDIENTS

1 banana
1 mango
1 cup pineapple
2 large apricots
2 cups baby spinach
¼ cup coconut flakes unsweetened
1/8 tsp nutmeg
1 cup hemp milk
1 cup distilled ice

ALOE GRAPES

INGREDIENTS

1 cup green grapes
2 apples
1 cup rapini
3 kiwi fruits
4 tablespoons aloe vera gel
1 cup hemp milk
1 cup distilled ice

WATER MELON SHAKE UP

INGREDIENTS

3 celery sticks
1 orange
1 cup romaine lettuce
3 cups water melon
1 light handful of mint leaves
1 sprig of lemon balm leaves
1 cup distilled water
1 cup distilled ice

LYCHEE DELICIOUS

INGREDIENTS

16 lychee fruits
1 cup radish greens
1 cup fresh pineapple
1 cup spinach
¼ cup watercress
1 cup brown rice milk
1 cup distilled ice

SESAME SEED STRAWBERRY

INGREDIENTS

1 1/2 cup strawberries
1 cup rocket leaves
1 cup orange segments
1 cup broccoli florets
24 grams golden sesame seeds
1 cup cashew milk unsweetened

BEETROOTED THE PRUNE

INGREDIENTS

1 cup chopped beetroot
1 cup prunes
1 cup broccoli
1 cup spinach
24 grams golden sesame seeds
1 cup hemp milk

WATERCRESS & THE MANGO TANGO

INGREDIENTS

2 ½ cups of watercress
1 cup ripe mango
1 cup chopped cauliflower florets
25 grams peanuts
1 cup brown rice milk

APRICOT DATES BROCCOLI

INGREDIENTS

1 cup apricots
½ cup dates
2 cups broccoli florets
24 grams chia seeds
1 cup chopped tomato
1 cup almond milk

BEETROOT GOJI BERRIES

INGREDIENTS

1 cup beetroot
½ cup goji berries
1 cup swiss chard
1 cup broccoli florets
25 grams almonds
1 cup almond milk

PECANED BY THE WATERCRESS

INGREDIENTS

2 cups rassberries
1 cup watercress
1 cup bok choy
25 gramd pecan nuts
½ tsp fresh ginger
1 cup coconut milk

CASHEWED THE CRANBERRY

INGREDIENTS

1 cup cranberries
1 avocado
1 cup baby spinach
1 cup fresh mint
25 grams cashew nuts
1 cup coconut milk

RED GRAPE RIPE FOR
GREEN CABBAGE

INGREDIENTS

1 cup green cabbage
2 cups red grapes
1 cup bok choy
20 gram pumpkin seeds
1/2 tsp whole grain mustard
1 cup cashew milk

AVOCADO PECAN

INGREDIENTS

1 ½ avocados
1 apple
1 cup green cabbage
1 cup mint
25 grams pecan nuts
1 cup coconut milk

PAPAYA FLAXED OUT

INGREDIENTS

2 cups papaya
1 cup broccoli florets
1 cup swiss chard
20 grams flax seeds
1 cup coconut water
1 squeeze of lime segment

BROCCOLIED THE GUAVA

INGREDIENTS

1 cup broccoli florets
1 cup papaya
1 cup swiss chard
¼ cup coriander
1 cup distilled water

BEETROOTS BLUEBERRY

INGREDIENTS

1 cup blueberries
1 cup chopped beetroot
2 cup broccoli florets
¼ cup cashew nuts
1 cup hemp milk

RED CABBAGE FENNEL OUT

INGREDIENTS

1 cup red cabbage
2 cups chopped pineapple
1 cup fennel
½ cup watercress
1 cup coconut water

AVOCADO GOES PAPYA

INGREDIENTS

1 cup papaya
1/2 cup blueberries
1 cup avocado
25 grams almond nuts
1 cup distilled water
1 cup distilled ice

CARROTS ON

INGREDIENTS

1 cup chopped carrot
1 cup broccoli florets
1 cup raspberries
1 cup swiss chard
1/8 cup coriander
1 cup almond milk

BROCCOLI AN GUAVA FIREWORKS

INGREDIENTS

1 ½ cup guava
1 cup chopped tomato
2 cup broccoli florets
10 gram pumpkin seeds
1 cup coconut water

GANESHAS GREEN TEA

INGREDIENTS

2 celery sticks
2 cups kale
2 cups ripe mango chopped
1 pear chopped
1 cup strong brewed green tea
1 cup distilled ice

SHIVAS BLUEBERRY BURST

INGREDIENTS

1 cup blueberries
2 green apples
1 cup spinach
1 cup romaine lettuce
½ tsp fresh ginger
5 gram pistasio nuts
1 cup coconut water
1 cup distilled ice

MELON OVER THE COCONUT

INGREDIENTS

1 cup baby spinach
2 1/2 cups honeydew melon
1/8 cup coconut grated flakes
1 cup coconut water
1 cup distilled water

PAIRED WITH AN APPLE

INGREDIENTS

1 apple
2 pears
1 cup baby spinach
1 tablespoon chia seeds
1 tablespoon sesame seeds
1 cup distilled water
1 cup distilled ice

LIMED OUT OF IT

INGREDIENTS

1 cup ripe red grapes
2 cups honeydew melon
1 apple
1 cup kale
¼ cup mint leaves
1 squeeze of lime segment
1 cup coconut water
1 cup distilled ice

GINGER APPLES

INGREDIENTS

1 cup lettuce
1 cup baby spinach
2 red apples
2 kiwis
1/2 tsp fresh ginger
1 big cucumber
1 cup distilled water

CACAO AN CARROT RAGE

INGREDIENTS

2 large carrots
1 cup of romaine lettuce
I cup cantaloupe melon
1 tsp raw organic cacao powder
1 cup almond coconut milk blend
1 cup coconut water
1 cup distilled ice

SESAME SEED FUSED FLAX SEED

INGREDIENTS

2 tablespoons flax seeds
1 tablespoon sesame seeds
1 cup lettuce
1 cup green grapes
1 green apple
1 cup distilled water
1 cup distilled ice

NUTTY NIVARNA

INGREDIENTS

1 cup cantaloupe melon
1 cup baby spinach
1 cup nectarines
10 grams macadamian nuts
10 grams pistachio nuts
1 cup distilled water
1 cup distilled ice

BOK CHOY GOES BANANAS

INGREDIENTS

2 bananas
1 cup bok choy
1 cup pineapple
1 cup rasspberies
½ cup tinned coconut milk
1 cup distilled water

APPLE PAIRED RED CABBAGE

INGREDIENTS

1 cup red cabbage
1 cup guava
1 cup baby spinach
1 green apple
¼ tsp cinnamon
25 grams hazel nuts
1 cup almond milk

PECAN AT THE PAPAYA

INGREDIENTS

1 1/4 cup papaya
1 cup goji berries
1 cup red grapes
1 cup green cabbage
25 grams pecan nuts
1 cup almond milk
½ cup hemp milk

MANGO AN PAPAYA ARE CUCUMBERED BY NUTMEG WHOS BANANAS

INGREDIENTS

1 cup mango
1 cup papaya
1 cup cucumber
1 banama
¼ tsp nutmeg
¼ tsp fresh ginger
1 cup coconut water

TOMATO TORUS STRAW FIELDS

INGREDIENTS

1 cup chopped tomatos
1 cup strawberries
1 cup broccoli florets
10 gram flax seeds
10 gram pistachio nuts
1 cup hemp milk

PRUNING AROUND NUTTY CACAO

INGREDIENTS

1 cup prunes
1 cup peaches
2 cup spinach
20 grams sesame seeds
¼ tsp cacao
½ cup coconut water
1 cup distilled water

PLUMING THE CASHEW

INGREDIENTS

1 cup chopped plums
1 cup green cabbage
1 cup guava
20 grams cashew nuts
5 grams poppy seeds
1 cup distilled water
1 cup almond milk

LUSCIOUS LYCHEE MANGOED

INGREDIENTS

1 cup bok choy
1 cup mango
12 lychee fruits
1 cup radish greens
½ cup pineapple
1 cup distilled water
1 cup distilled ice

BROCCOLI GRAPED KIWI

INGREDIENTS

1 cup sweet green grapes
1 green apple
1 cup broccoli
2 kiwi fruits
I cup hemp milk
1 cup ginger green tea brewed

NUTRITIOUS SOUPS
FOR THE CELLS OF YOUR BIOLOGY

ALSO
PUFFY NAAN BREAD WRAPS
& RICE PAPER ROLLS

SWEET POTATO, SQUASH
& COCONUT SOUP

Preparation time 10 minutes
Cooking time 40 minutes
Serves 4

Ingredients

1 large butternut squash peeled diced
2 large sweet potatos peeled diced
2 garlic cloves peeled
1 onion cut in wedges
2 tablespoons olive oil

1 tsp cumin seeds
900ml of gluten free vegetable stock
1 tsp sea salt
1 tsp black pepper
1 tsp chilli flakes
200ml coconut cream

Preheat oven to 200c take baking tray line with baking paper and put the garlic, squash, sweet potatos, onion, then sprinkle cumin seeds over the top of the vegtables, they are ready when golden and still tender. Mix in the remaining ingredients heat through and then put in blender until smooth.

Serve with a garnish of chill flakes and accompany with vegan naan bread.

The above recipe can be changed slightly by removing the sweet potato and replacing them with split red lentils, roast the vegtables for twenty minutes then put in pot add 100grams of red lentils, gluten free vegetable stock then simmer for 25 minutes then when squash and lentils are soft, put in blender then serve with a home made vegan gluten free bread.

TOMATO BASIL & RED PEPPER SOUP

Preparation time 10 minutes
Cooking time 25 minutes
Serves 4

INGREDIENTS

500 grams red pepper
1 big onion
2 garlic cloves
2 tablespoons olive oil
1 tsp paprika
1 tsp cumin
600 ml gluten free vegaeable stock
500 grams tomatos
1/2 cup parsley

Preparation

Put the red peppers on baking paper on a
baking tray drizzle olive oil over peppers, cook
at 200c for 12 minutes.

Get large sauce pan and put olive oil, garlic, onion, cook for 4 minutes until unions soft, add tomatos, black pepper and salt seasoning.

Then remove peppers from oven, skin them chop up then add in soup cooking for further 15 minutes, then take off stove and let cool for 5 minutes, then roughly blend in blender and serve with parsley garnish on top of soup.

VIETNAMESE RICE PAPER ROLLS

Preparation time 15 minutes
Serves 12 rolls

INGREDIENTS

¼ big cucumber
1 cup corriander
¼ cup mint
1/4 cup thai basil
150 grams cooked rice vermicelli noodles
cold.

¼ iceberg lettuce thinly sliced
12 rice paper sheets round
Lime segment squeeze to serve

Dipping sauce

1 tablespoon toasted sesame seeds
2 tablespoons home made sweet chilli
sauce
Juice of 1 lime
2 tablespoon aminos coconut dressing

PREPERATION

Now mix in bowl the herbs, cucumber,
rice noodles, and lettuce, then soak rice
paper in a prepared bowl of warm water
for 20 seconds then drain on kitchen
paper, now spoon the mixture on to the
centre of rice paper leaving an 25mm at
top and bottom, so you can wrap ends in
as you roll it together, repeat with all
other 11 rice paper veg rolls.

Then whisk the dipping sauces
ingredients together and serve in small

bowl and serve with thr Vietnamese veg
rice rolls accompanied by some lime
segments, wedges.

MEXICAN BEAN SOUP

Preparation time 10 minutes
Cooking time 30 minutes
Serves 4

INGREDIENTS

1 garlic clove crushed
1 onion chopped
1 tablespoon olive oil
½ cup coriander plus chopped stalks
1 red chill
1 tsp ground cumin
1 green pepper
400 grams chopped tomato
800 grams of black eyed beans
Seasoning black pepper & sea salt
2 tablespoon sun dried tomatos
600 ml gluten free vegetable stock

Preparation

Heat the olive oil in pan put in the onion,
garlic, chilli for 2 minutes add the
coriander and the chopped stalks that are
rich in flavour, and add green peppers the
stir then add the cumin and paprika.

Then stir in the tomatos the beans and stock and bring to boil and simmer 20 minutes.

Then let cool 5 minutes then put half of the pan soup contents into blender and and blend then return to the pan puur in the blended half bean soup stir, serve in bowls and garnish with coriander leaves.

If you wish to have a side dish then make guacamole, get a bowl smash up large avocado squeeze juice of 1 lime in, put in 3 chopped spring onions, add sea salt, 1 small chilli finely sliced and then coriander chopped leaves and stir, side plate readt to go.

CHIPOTLE CHILLI SAUCE OR SOUP

Preparation 20minutes
Cooking 45 minutes
Serves 6

INGREDIENTS

5 chipotle chillies
500 grams tomatos
1 tsp dried oregano
150 ml red wine
3 garlic cloves chopped
1 tsp French whole grain mustard
½ tsp ground fresh black pepper corns
4 ½ tablespoons clear honey
½ tsp sea salt

Preparation

Put oven on 200c put tomatos in baking tray cook for 45 minutes until charred, soak the chillies in water for 18 minutes until soft, no seed just chilli flesh and chop up chillies.

Remove tomatos from oven let cool then remove skins, put tomatos in blender add chillies and the garlic and red wine, then add the sea salt, pepper, whole grain mustard and oregano then blend.

Pour out blender into pan and bring to a simmer for 10 minutes stir and pour in bowls for serving, and add garnish oregano herb leave in centre of bowl.

RED LENTIL & COCONUT
SPICY SOUP

Preparation time 20 minutes
Cooking time 45 minutes
Serves 4

INGEDIENTS

2 red onion chopped fine
1 chilli finely sliced use seeds as well
2 tablespoons sesame seed oil
1 lemon grass stick take off outer layer
and chop very fine
2 garlic cloves
1 cup red lentils
1 tsp paprika
1 tsp coriander ground
3 ½ cups distilled water
1 ¾ cups coconut milk canned
3 spring onions
½ cup fresh cirander leaves

½ tsp sea salt
½ tsp black pepper
Juice 1 lime

Preparation

Put oil in pan to heat then add garlic, onion, lemon grass, chilli, stir and cook for 6 mins until soft not golden, por in the cocont milk and water add the spices, sea salt & black pepper and red lentils.
Stir let it simmer for 40 minutes until lentils are mushy.
Then stir in sring onions, coriander and lime juice stir and ready to put in bowls and serve it with garnish coriander leaves in centre of the bowl. Also home made vegan sundried naan bread goes so well with this.

PUFFY NAAN WRAPS

Puffy vegan naan wraps gluten free and yeast free prepared in only 20 minutes, the reward when made is a balanced puffy naan wrap, that is ready to go with a variety of snack dips or starters and main courses.

Preparation time 10 minutes
Cook time 10 minutes
Total time 20 minutes

Ingredients

1 tsp sesame seed oil
½ tsp sea salt or Himalayan salt
½ to ¾ cup coconut milk
¼ cup coconut or plain yogurt
2 tsp baking powder
½ cup of arrowroot starch
1.2 cup potato starch
2 gloves garlic
½ cup coconut flour

Options to serve with coriander, parsley, crushed garlic, sundried tomato, vegan butter, olive oil.

Serving 10 mini naan or 5 big naan

Instructions

Use a mixing bowl add the coconut milk, baking powder, coconut yougut, sesame seed oil, garlic and sea salt and stir and combine by whisking well. The mixture will puff up and become frothy if your plain yogurt is live with active cultures.

Then add into the mixing bowl the potato starch, arrowroot starch and coconut flour and stir mixture to combine, it will form a malleable, moist dough it should not split when rolled if so add more coconut milk, and should not be gummy if it is add more potato starch.

Your rolling board should be dusted with flour dust the dough with flour, using the rolling pin roll into an oval or round shape to about 5 mm thick.

Then heat your pan to just above medium heat temperature drizzle with olive oil, then gently place raw naan in pan, now cook for 3 minutes on each side, if you like a puffy naan then use medium heat and cook silently less on each side till its just golden in colour. If you have any to cook repeat the same process.

To serve add your preffered toppings, herbs, crushed garlic, sundried tomatos, with a light drizzle of oil.

TOFU CHOWDER SOUP

Preparation time 10 minutes
Cooking time 30 minutes
Serve 4

INGREDIENTS

1 onion finely chopped
3 tablespoon sunflower oil
14 grams vegan butter
600 ml vegan vegetable stock
2 tablespoons tapioca flour or corn flour
600 ml coconut cream milk canned
500 grams potatoes diced
½ tsp black pepper
1/2 tsp sea salt
12 oz tofu (3oz serving per person) cut up in small cubes
150ml vegan cream home made mixed soy milk with olive oil.
¼ cup fresh parsley herb

Preperations

Heat a pan up put vegan butter, sunflower oil,
add the onion and cook till soft for 6 minutes,
also put on another pan and add 2 tablespoon of
oil and heat up put tofu in pan, turning on all 6
sides till lighly golden, then in other pan add in
the flour of your two choices, stir for 30
seconds add the coconut milk, vegan vegetable
stock, when thickened add potatoes and simmer
for 9 minutes then add the tofu and cook for 6
minutes, mix in the home made soy milk/olive
oil cream and cook further 3-5 minutes.
Take of stove pour in 4 bowls and garnish with
parsley, and vegan home made garlic naan go
well with this tofu chowder.
This can also be a Spiced tofu chowder just add
1-2 yellow chilles freshly sliced no seeds.

A GAZPACO COOLED SOUP

Preparation time 20 minutes
Chilling time period
Serves 6

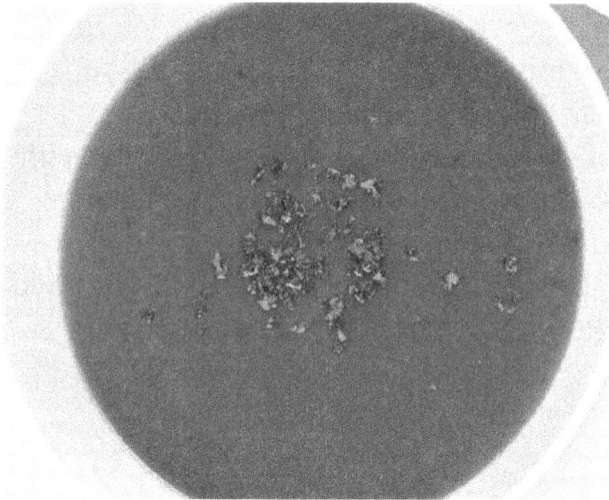

INGREDIENTS

½ large cucumber chopped
885 grams tomatos skinned
1 celery stick chopped

2 red peppers chopped
½ red chilli sliced no seed
2 cloves garlic sliced
2 tablespoons white wine vinegar
¼ cup coriander leaves
4 tablespoons sesame seed
2 tablesoons olive oil
½ tsp sea salt
2 tablespoons sundried tomato paste
4 tablespoon chia seeds
18 distilled ice cubes to serve

Preparation

Get bowl mix all vegtables together then chilli,
Garlic, coriander, then add sundried tomato
paste, sesame seed oil, vinegar and sea salt and
put in blender till smooth, check salt content to
your taste then cover and put in fridge for 12-24
hours.

To serve Gazpacho topping heat 2 tablespoons
olive oil in pan 160 grams gluten free tapioca
bread cubes, fry till golden on all sides, put in
bowls and add 2 chopped up spring onions

divided in each bowl, add a finely sliced green pepper, chopped coriander leaf, 4 tablespoon chia seeds divided in bowels.

You can also add tofu cubes after 6-10 minutes in pan of olive oil cooking till golden on all 6 sides, then add to soup.

To serve pour in bowls put few distilled ice cubes in each dish equal distance, put toppings in soup and garnish with coriander leaf.

COCONUT & PUMPKIN SOUP

Preparation time 20
Cooking time 25 minutes
Serves 4

INGREDIENTS

4 shallots chopped
2 garlic cloves crushed
1 lemon grass stick chopped
1 tablespoon sundried tomato paste
450 grams pumpkin cut in cubcs
2 green chilli plus seeds
2 red chilli plus seeds
600 ml vegan vegetable stock
600 ml coconut cream milk canned or a block
2 tablespoons soy sauce
1 tsp coconut sugar
¼ cup chopped basil leafs to garnish
1 tsp black ground pepper
1 tsp fresh grated ginger
1tsp sea salt

Preperations

Now grind to paste the lemon grass, green
chillies, shallots, sea salt, garlic, sundried
tomato paste, then put vegan vegetable stock in
pan bring to boil add the mixed paste stir till
blended, then add pumpkin cook on simmer for
12 minutes until pumpkin soft, then add the
coconut cream, soy sauce, ginger and black
pepper. Cook for further 13 minutes then take
off heat.

To serve pour in bowls garnish with bail leaves,
the puffy garlic naan goes well with this dish.

TOMATO AND BASIL SOUP

Preparation time ten minutes
Cooking time ten minutes
Serves 4

INGEDIENTS

1 cup basil chopped
½ tsp sea salt
½ tsp black pepper
600 grams tomatos
1200 ml distilled water
4 tablespoon coconut thick cream tinned
Preparation

Put all ingredients in blender apart from coconut cream and small bit basil to garnish, mix in blender till smooth, then pour in pan heat for ten minutes, then take off heat.

To serve pour in bowls garnish with basil, and place a tablespoon of coconut cream in centre of bowl. This is nice with sundried tomato puffy naan bread.

MISO & TOFU SOUP

Preperation time 20 minutes
Cooking time 15 minutes
Serves 4

INGREDIENTS

1 spring onion chopped
2 tablespoons wakame seaweed
3 tablespoons miso soya bean seasoning
½ tsp Sichuan peppercorn
125 grams tofu diced tiny
500 ml distilled water
½ cup shitake mushrooms
1 tablespoon sesame seed oil

This below is blended into one vegan dashi
2 tablspoon tapacio flour
450 ml distilled water
½ cup shitake mushrooms chopped
2 tablespoons kombu dried kelp

First get the blender and add 450 ml distilled water, ½ cup mushrooms, kombu kelp, tapacio flour bend till smooth.

Soak your wakame seadweed for 12 minutes then drain and cut into small pieces.

Now put pan on heat put in sesame seed oil and cook tofu on all 6 cube sides till golden brown.

Now put pan on again put 500 ml water with aal other ingredients in on top part ingedients list bring to boil let simmer then add vegan dasi sauce when hot take of heat and serve in bowl.

Can serve with a vegan bread.

HEATHLY SALADES

RAW FOODS MEAN MORE LIGHT FOR YOUR CELLS

CHICKPEA AVOCADO & VEGAN CHEESE SALADE

Preparation time 10 minutes
Cooking time 12 minutes
Serves 4

INGREDIENTS

150 gram crumbled vegan cheese
500 gram red peppers in halfs
800 grams chickpeas
4 tablespoon olive oil
90 grams rocket leaves
1 red chilli sliced no seeds
125 gram red cherry tomatoes cut to 1/8th s
¼ tsp black pepper
1 cup coriander
½ cup chopped mint
Drizzles of red wine vinegar
¼ avocado

Preparation

Get baking paper put on a baking tray lay red pepper halfs down then drizzle oil over them, cook on 200c 10 minutes 5 minutes each side then peel off skins, cut avocado up.
Place peppers in bowls add chickpeas, vegan cheese, rocket leaves, chilli, herbs, avocado and tomatos then mix together, now drizzle red wine vinegar over the salads to finish.

AVOCADO & POTATO SALAD

Preparation time 10 minutes
Cooking time 12 minutes
Serves 4

INGREDIENTS

1 ripe avocado
1/2 cup cress
½ cup mustard leaves
600 grams baby potatoes
90 grams rockert leaves
½ lemon non waxed grated rind
½ tablespoon black pepper
½ tablespoon sea salt

Salade dressing

½ juice lemon
1 tablespoon whole grain French mustard
2 tablespoon hummus

Preparation

Cook the potatos in pan water with mint leaves for 15-20 minutes, drain put in bowl, cut the adocado into small cubes, mix the dressing up then put potatoes in bowel add the salad, and the lemon hommus dressing on top, then serve.

Alternitavely you can add 8 large sundried tomatos cut up, 12 green olives, 4 large tablespoons thick coconut cream and 2 table spoons of pesto.

PEAR WALNUT & GREEN SALAD

Preparation time 10 minutes
Cooking time 3 minutes
Serves 4

INGREDIENTS

130 gram mixed green leaves
55 grams walnuts pieces toasted
2 big ripe pears
2 tablespoon olive oil
70 grams vegan cheese cut into strips

Sadad dressing

2 tablespoon lemon juice
1 tabespoon whole grain French mustard
2 tablespoon agave necture
6 tablespoon walnut oil
3 tarragon sprigs chopped
½ tsp sea salt
½ tsp black pepper

Preparation

Get baking tray line with baking paper lay out drizzle olive oil over cheese cook under hot grill for 3 minutes turning half way through grilling until golden crisp, take out let cool and cut into croutes.

Now make dressing put ingredients in large bowl and mix, half pears and cut into slices, then add them to bowl with salad leaves, walnuts, add dressing toss salad then add vegan golden crispy cheese croutes, ready to serve.

QUINOA & ROASTED VEGGIE SALAD

Preparation time 5 minutes
Cooking time 20 minutes
Serves 4

INGREDIENTS

2 red peppers chopped
3 courgettes chopped
1 big aubergine chopped
2 red onions chopped
3 garlic cloves chopped
2 tabespoons green pesto
160 grams quinoa
3 tablespoon olive oil
90 grams rocket leaves
1 tablespoon balsamic vinegar

Preparation

Put oven on get baking tray line with baking
paper lay out vegtables drizzle with olive oil

Then cook at 220c for 22 minutes.
Then cook quinoa in pan boiling water till
cooked then drain, get small bowl mix pesto
balsamic vinegar then put roasted vegtables in
bowls with quinoa and rocket leaves, stir salad
and serve warm.

Alternitavely you can add sundried tomato
paste instead of pesto and use watercress
instead of rocket.

CUCUMBER & CASHEW SALAD

Preparation time ten minutes
Cooking time none
Serves 4

INGREDIENTS

6 cup rocket leaves
6 cup baby spinach leaves
1 large cucumber
½ tsp sea salt gound
½ tsp black pepper ground
3 tablespoon coconut aminos dressing
4 tablespoon sesame seed oil
1 tablespoon whole grain French mustard
1 cup cashew nuts
½ cup watercress leaves garnish

Preparation

Put salade leaves in large bowl cut up cucumber
Add to bowel with cashew nuts, then add
French mustard, coconut aminos dressing, sea

salt, black pepper then drizzle sesame seed oil over and toss salade, then serve in 4 bowls adding watercress garnish.

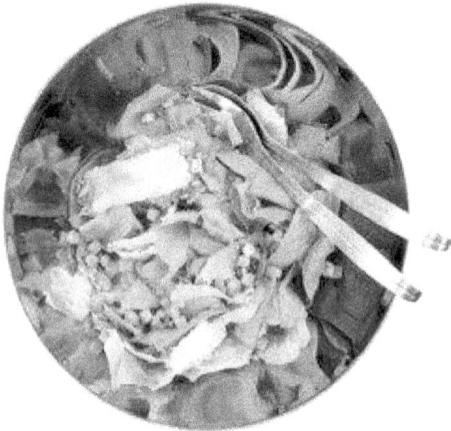

SPRING ONION & MACADAMIA SALAD

Preparation time 10 minutes
Cooking none
Serves 4

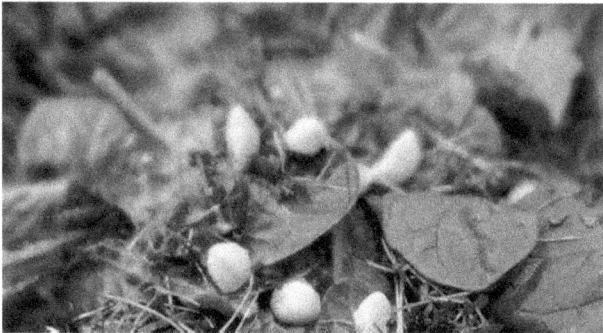

INGREDIENTS

4 cups baby spinach leaves
2 cups rocket leaves
1 cup coriander leaves

4 big spring onions
1 cup plain macadamia nuts no salt
½ tsp groung black pepper
6 tablespoon pumpkin seed oil
½ tsp sea salt

Preparation

Get 4 bowls divide all 3 salad leaves into four put in bowls, at spring onion, macadamia nuts, sea salt and black pepper then drizzle pumpkin seed oil over 4 salad bowls, ready to serve.

GREEN BEAN & GINGER SALAD

Preparation time 10 minutes
Cooking time 15 minutes
Serves 4

INGREDIENTS

6 cups cos lettuce chopped
6 tablespoon hazel nut oil
4 cups green beans
4 tablespoons fresh grated ginger
4 tablespoon pine nuts
½ tsp sea salt
½ tablespoon black pepper

Preparation

Bring water in pan to boil place green beans in pan and cook high heat for 15 minutes, then drain and put on plate.

Get 4 bowls divide cos lettuce even put in bowls along with green beans add fresh ginger, pine nuts, sea salt, black pepper, then drizzle 4 bowls with hazel nut oil, and serve.

BEETROOT & MUSHROOM SALAD

Preparation time 20 minutes
Cooking time 30 minutes
Serves 4

INGREDIENTS

6 cup rocket leaves
3 cup romaine leaves
2 beetroots
2 cup shitake mushrooms chopped
½ tsp sea salt
½ tsp black pepper
¼ tsp cayenne chilli pepper
6 tablespoons rapeseed oil

Preparation

Get pan fill with water bring to boil drop in beetroots and boil for 30 minutes, drain and put on cutting board and dice to small cubes, while bean cooking put 1 tablespoon oil in pan till hot then add shitake mushrooms for ten minutes and remove from pan, then get 4 bowls divine 2 salad leaves evenly then add the beetroot, shitake mushrooms, sea salt and 2 peppers, then drizzle the rapeseed oil over the 4 salad bowls and serve.

ORANGE GINGER TOFU SALAD

Preparation time 10 minutes
Cooking time 10 minutes
Serves 4

INGREDIENTS

1 large sweet orange need juice & rind
4 tablespoons fresh grated ginger
150 grams tofu cut into cubes
6 cups radicchio red leaves
1 cup coriander leaves
½ tsp Himalayan pink salt
½ tsp cayenne chilli pepper
6 tablespoon avocado oil

Preparation

Put pan on heat add 1 tablespoon avocado oil
then add tofu cubes and cook for ten minutes
till all 6 sides golden then remove from pan.

Lay 4 bowls out add the 2 salade leaves then add the grated ginger, Himalayan sea salt, the cayenne pepper and tofu. Then take ring off orange put even in bowls then squeeze orange juice over salad then drizzle the avocado oil over to, ready to serve.

APPLE WALNUT & VEGAN CHEESE SALAD

Preparation time ten minutes
Cooking time 10 minutes
Serves 4

INGREDIENTS

2 red apples chopped then sliced
1 cup chopped walnuts
2 cup vegan cheese
6 cup romaine leaves
2 cup watercress leaves
½ tsp himalayan pink salt
½ tsp white pepper corns crushed
6 tablespoons pine seed oil

Preparation

Get pan put on heat add 1 tablespoon of pine
nut oil and place chopped cubed vegan cheese
in cook until all 6 sides are golden, remove
from pan, get 4 bowls divide 2 salad leaves

evenly then add the apples, walnuts, Himalayan pink salt, crushed white pepper, then add the crispy golden vegan cheese, now add a drizzle of pine seed oil over top salade in 4 bowls, ready to serve.

HEALTHY MAIN COURSES

TO FEED YOUR BIOLOGICAL CELLS

CHILLI RICE NOODLES

Preparation time 10 minutes
Cooking time 10 minutes
Serves 4

INGREDIENTS

2 tablespoons gluten free soy sauce
2 tablespoons agave syrup
2 tsp sundried tomato paste
8 tsp rice vinegar
225 grams rice ribbon noodles
1 red chilli no seed sliced
2 tablespoon sesame seed oil
120 grams mangetout peas sliced
1 big red pepper sliced
¼ tsp sea salt

Preparation

Get mixing bowl put in sundried tomato paste, vinegar, soy sauce and agave syrup mix well, then put noodles in pan boiling water with sea salt for 6-8 minutes unti soft. While that's cooking get pan heat sesame seed oil then put in red chilli, red pepper and peas and cook for 5 minutes. Add noodles and vinegar to vegetable pan cook for 2 minutes, then ready to serve in 4 bowls.

AUBERGINE BAKE

Preparation time 10 minutes
Cooking time 40 minutes
Serves 4

INGREDIENTS

160 grams grated vegan cheese
2 big aubergine chopped
2 tablespoons olive oil
¼ tsp black gound pepper
¼ tsp sea salt

Tomato sauce

1 garlic clove crushed
1 tablespoon olive oil
¼ cup chopped basil
420 grams plum tomatos
1 onion finely chopped

Preperations

To make the tomato sauce heat oil in pan add onions, galic fry for 4 minutes till soft then add basil, tomatos and simmer for 12 minutes.

Then brush the aubergine with olive oil and cook on griddle pan, for 2 minutes each side until charred brown.
Now get a cooking glass tray put some sauce in then layer the aubergine on top then add half the vegan cheese, repeat the layering process again finish with vegan cheese on the top.
Put in oven on 200c for 20 minutes until top is golden, remove from oven serve on 4 plates.
Can serve with a salad and naan bread of your choosing.

POTATO MARGHERITA PIZZA

Preparation time 20 minutes
Cooking time 40 minutes
Serves 3

INGREDIENTS

1 kg baked potatoes sliced
175 gram vegan cheese
4 tablespoon sundried tomato paste
3 tablespoons olive oil
500 grams cherry tomatos
1 1/2 tablespoons chopped thyme
1 tablespoon chopped oregano
1 tablespoon tapioca starch & 3 tablespoon
distilled water instead of egg

Preparation

Bring pan water to boil put potatoes in boil for
18 minutes, drain and put back in pan, add 2
tablespoon oil, tapioca starch, half vegan
cheese, mix well.

Then get baking tray lined with baking paper and pour pan contents onto tray spreading out to size of a pizza then bake at 200c for 12 minutes, then remove from oven spread tomato paste over evenly then lay out tomato slices and finish with vegan cheese then sprinkle the oregano and thyme herbs on top, drizzle olive oil over potato pizza then cook for further 10-14 minutes remove from oven slice portions out and serve on plate.

This goes well with my pear and walnut salad.

SPINACH & NUT PIE

Preparation time 10 minutes
Cooking time 40 minutes
Serves 2-4

INGREDIENTS

1/2 cup oine nuts
½ cup cashew nuts
½ cup brasil nuts
1 tablespoon olive oil
1 onion chopped
180 gram spinach leaf
45 grams vegan butter
28 grams rice flour
600 ml coconut canned milk
1 tablespoon whole grain mustard
1 tsp nutmeg
¼ tsp sea salt
¼ tsp black pepper

Potato crust topping

100 ml coconut cream
1 tablespoon vegan butter
1 kg potatoes chopped

Preparation

First cook the potatoes in pan boiling water for 16 minutes, drain return to pan add coconut cream, vegan butter, sea salt, black pepper mix then put aside off heat.
Get another pan put oil, onions cook for 3 minutes then add the spinach till wilted then add butter, coconut milk, flour mix then add the nutmeg and mustard mix well then add all 3 types of nuts in.
Then put in glass oven dish spread out even then add potatoes in top layering them cook for 15-18 minutes then remove from oven and serve on 4 plates. My green bean and ginger salad goes very well with this dish.

CHILLI TOMATO & OKRA

Preparation time 15 minutes
Cooking time 20 minutes
Serves 4

INGREDIENTS

2 onions chopped
6 tomatoes
2 garlic cloves sliced
1 green chilli with seeds
360 grams okra (marrow family)
1 juice of lemon
2 tablespoon olive oil
170 ml distilled water
¼ cup coriander chopped
1 tablespoon paprika

Preparation

Get a chopping board cut okra to small pieces,

and the tomatos as well, then put in blender garlic a cut up onion, paprika, 4 tablespoons water, coriander and blend to paste.

Heat thr olive oil in pan slice the second onion into rings anf fry till golden brown for 5 minutes, then place onion rings on paper on plate to drain.

Now put blended paste in pan cook for two minutes on a lower heat then add tomatoes, lemon juice, okra and distilled water left mix well then let simmer for 14 minutes till okra soft.

Then serve on plate with onion rings on top as garnish. If you need a filling meal then add leeks and aubergine.

RED CURRIED GREEN BEAN
& BEANCURD

Preparation time 10 minutes
Cooking time 10 minutes
Serves 4

INGREDIENTS

118 grams trimmed green beans
230 grams portobello mushrooms
180 grams beancurd tofu cut in small cubes
3 tablespoon sundried tomato paste
2 tablespoon coconut sugar
620 ml coconut cream milk
1 tablespoon of red curry paste
½ cup coriander garnish
2 red chillies with seeds
3 split lime leaves

Preparation

Get pan put curry paste, coconut milk, coconut sugar and mix then add the rest of milk and mushrooms stir then let simmer to boil.
Now add the tofu beancurd and green beans let simmer 4 minutes mix in the lime leaves then the chillies cook for minute then serve adding coriander garnish on top.

ROOT VEGTABLE SPICEY GRATIN

Preparation time 25 minutes
Cooking time 1hr 45 minutes
Serves 4

INGREDIENTS

285 grams sweet potatoes
180 grams celeriac
450 gram potatoes
160 ml coconut milk
¼ cup chopped parsley garnish
¼ tsp sea salt
¼ tsp black pepper
140 ml coconut cream
4 shallots chopped
1 tsp coriander
1 tsp chilli powder
1 tsp turmeric
1 tablespoon unsalted vegan butter
1 tsp curry powder

Preparation

Slice celeriac, sweet potatoes, potatoes thinly put in bowl of water to stop discolouring, put oven on to 180c, get pan heat curry powder and half the vegan butter, coriander then add half the chilli powder mix cook for two minutes, then let sit to cool.
Now drain water from vegetable slices and place in cooking dish and add the shallots and spice mix in mixing together.
Now add sea salt, black pepper to each layer layed for balanced seasoning, mix the coconut milk and cream together and pour over the gratin and sprinkle the rest of chilli on top.
Cover with baking foil and cook for 40 minutes, then remove the foil add last of butter to top of gratin and cook for further 50 minutes until golden brown and crisp.
Now serve on plates and add the parsley herb garnish on top and serve.

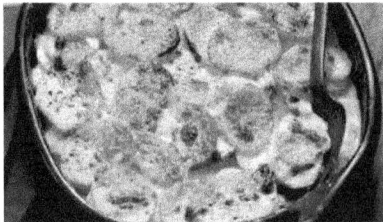

LEMON & GINGER CHILL BEANS

Preparation time 15 minutes
Cooking time 20 minutes
Serves 4

INGREDIENTS

3 garlic cloves chopped
1 tablespoon sunflower oil
260 ml distilled water
Large piece of fresh ginger 55mm chopped
1 chilli sliced no seed
1 onion chopped
1 tsp ground coriander
1 tsp cayenne pepper
1 tsp ground cumin
2 tablespoon lemon juice
1 tsp ground turmeric
1 ½ cup chopped coriander leave
400 grams haricot beans
400 grams aduki beans
400 grams black eyed beans
¼ tsp black gound pepper

Preparation

Get blender put in 4 ½ tablespoons of water
adding garlic, ginger blend till smooth, get pan
heat oil add chilli, onion stir cook 5 minutes till
golden, add the coriander, turmeric, cumin,
cayenne pepper and stir for 1 minute.
Now stir in garlic, ginger paste cook for 1 more
minute, add remaining water fresh coriander,
lemon juice mixing and bring to the boil, cook
for 5 minutes with lid on pan.
Then stir in all 3 bean types and cook for a
further 8 minutes, then serve in bowls and
garnish with fresh coriander leaves. A nice
vegan bread goes well with this dish to soak the
juices. Can add a vegan coconut cream to serve.

RED & GREEN CHILLI SPLIT PEAS

Preparation time 10 minutes
Cooking time 12 minutes
Serves 4

INGREDIENTS

2 onions chopped
1 tablespoon fresh grated ginger
1 piece cinnamon bark
1 bay leaf
2 tablespoon rapeseed oil
120 grams yellow split peas
2 garlic cloves
2 red chillies no seed
2 green chillies no seed
1 ½ tablespoon fresh cut mint

Preparation

Get bowl cold water put split peas in cover
30mm over top split peas, leave to soak over

night. Then drain them boil them till they split and are soft and put aside.

Put oil in pan on medium heat put in onions, cinnamon bark, bay leaf then add garlic, ginger, and half red chillies and half green chillies, then drain split peas and add to pan adding mint and rest og red and green chillies, mix a minute and serve in bowls.

CHILLI JAM
WITH COURGETTE FRITTERS

Preparation time 20 minutes
Cooking time 35 minutes
Makes 12 fritters

INGREDIENTS

Chilli jam

2 chillies no seeds
2 tablespoons coconut sugar
4 onions chopped
4 garlic cloves chopped
6 tablespoon rapeseed oil

Courgette fritters

½ tsp sea salt
½ tsp black ground pepper
4 tablespoon sunflower oil
55 grams vegan cheese grated
4 tablespoon tapacio flour
460 grams courgette grated
2 tablespoon flax seed &
6 tablespoon of distilled water (no eggs)

Preperations

Make the chilli jam heat oil in pan add garlic
onions and cook for 18 minutes until soft, leave
to cool then put in blender add coconut sugar,
chillies and blend then return to pan cook for 10
minutes.

Making the fritters squeeze courgettes in tea
towel to remove excess water put in bowl add
the vegan cheese, tapacio flour, flax seed,
distilled water mix and add sea salt, black
pepper.

Now heat the oil in pan put in 2 tablespoon of
mixture for each fritter, cook for 2 ½ minutes
each side, then drain them on kitchen paper,
then serve on plate with chilli jam.

VEGAN
DESSERTS & COOKIES

PUMPKIN CHOCOLATE
CHIP COOKIES

These pumpkin cookies with oats and vegan cacao chocolate chips, they are naturally gluten free so therefore vegan they are a wholesome snack when you get the munchies.

Preperation time 45 minutes
Cook time 15 minutes
Total time 1 hour

Ingredients
¼ cup grated dried coconut flesh
¾ cup oats rolled
3/4 cup almond flour
¾ tsp baking powder
¼ sea salt
¼ cup chick pea brine

2 tsp pumpkin butter
3rd cup cacao chocolate chips
½ cup coconut sugar
2 tbsp coconut oil
½ tsp vanilla extract
1¼ tbsp pumpkin spice

Serving 12 cookies

Instructions

Use a mixing bowel mix together oats, coconut, almond flour, cacao chocolate chips, baking powder, sea salt, pumpkin spice, coconut sugar, baking powder.

Then in another bowl whisk the chick pea brine when fluffy, then add the vanilla, pumpkin butter, oil and whisk till it has combined then add the other ingredients and mix them till they combine as one, it should of formed to a dough.

Wrap in cling film and put in fridge for 25 minutes or you can leave over night for convenience.

Heat oven to 175c and put baking paper on your cooking tray, use aproxemately 2 ½ table spoon amounts of chilled dough and flatten them till round then put them on baking paper on the baking tray 25mm apart.

Bake for 15 minutes until they have expanded and are golden crispy, remove from the oven take them off the cooking tray onto a rack to cool for 5-10 minutes.

Then ready to go, serve up they will be munched up rapido.

CARAMAL SALTY CASHEW BALLS

These caramal salty cashew balls are easy to make with only 4 ingredients needed for a healthly munchie, the flavours of caramal, coconut and with the sea salt and cashew nuts the mouth waters then the taste buds dance.

Preparation time 10 minutes
Total time 10 minutes

Ingredients

¼ tsp sea salt
1/3 cup roasted unsalted cashew nuts
¼ cup unsweetened grated coconut
1 cup chopped dates
Serving 10 balls

preperations

Use a mixing processor, add to the bowl
cashews, coconut, sea salt and dates, mix until
it has blended and formed into a dough, mix for
about a minute if its splitting add more dates or
a nut butter.

Now ready portion out into ten even balls and
serve I can guarantee they will be munched
quickly.

CHILLI CACAO PLANTAIN CHIPS

Preparation time 5 minutes
Cooking time 10 minutes
Serves 4

INGREDIENTS

Sesame seed oil for frying
2 big very ripe plantains
1 tsp ground cinnamon
½ tsp chlli powder
1 tsp cacao powder

preperation

Peel plantains slice them diagonally 10mm
thick, put oil in pan 10mm deep to fry
plantains, drop in they should float to surface
and bubble straight away.
Cook till they are golden brown in colour then
put on kitchen paper to drain, then put in a bowl
and mix in chilli powder, cacao powder and
cinnamon spice, they are now ready plate and
serve. These go well with a lime vegan ice
cream.

PISTACHIO LEMON & FRUIT SQUARES

Preparation time 10 minutes
Cooking time 20 minutes
Makes 16 servings

INGREDIENTS

74 grams pistachio nuts unsalt
74 grams almond flakes
120 grams coconut sugar
145 grams millet flakes
Vegan butter used for greasing
1 lemon grind
80 grams dried dates
400 grams coconut milk
42 grams corn flakes gluten free
12 grams sunflower seeds
12 grams pumpkin seeds

Preparation

Get a bowl and mix the ingredients until combined, then grease tray with vegan butter, put mix in oven at 180c for 20 minutes, then remove cool for 5 minutes and serve.

MINI MINCE PIES

Preparation time 10 minutes
Cooking time 18 minutes
Makes 24 mini mince pies

INGREDIENTS

Mince filling

26 grams vegan marzipan grated
1 ½ tablespoons brandy
26 grams almond flakes chopped
410 grams mincemeat gluten free

Crust pastry

1 grated orange rind
2 tablespoons coconut sugar
76 grams vegan butter
155 grams rice flour
¼ tsp cinnamon
2 tablespoons
1 tablespoon flax seed &
3 tablespoons distilled water (instead of egg)

Preparation

Get a blender put in cinnamon, polenta, flour
until looks like bread crumbs, add the flax seed,

3 tablespoons water and mix to paste then wrap in film and put in fridge for 25 minutes.
Get a board and rolling pin flour board and then roll to 5mm thick, then cut 24 circles to 60mm wide put in line the mini trays and then fill with mixture.

Put oven on at 180c put in cook for 18 miniutes until golden, remove from oven let stand for 5 minutes and serve. You can make them thicker and creamier by adding 2 ½ tablespoons of whipped tofu, ½ tablespoon coconut cream and 1 tablespoon of brandy, then put tofu in bottom of pastries and mince filling on top.

MANGO FLAPJACKS

Preparation time 10 minutes
Cooking time 30 minutes
Makes 12 mango flapjacks

INGREDIENTS

2 tablespoons agave syrup
155 grams vegan butter
100 grams coconut sugar
80 grams dried mango chopped
1 tablespoon sunflower seeds
1 tablespoons pumpkin seeds
200 grams millet flakes

Preperations

Get baking tray greese with vegan butter then
get pan heat butter, coconut sugar, agave syrup
and stir and melt, then mix in rest of ingredients
put in tray put in oven on 150c for 28 minutes,
remove from oven then stand for 5 minutes
before serving. You can adapt recipes as I do
blueberry and almound, hazelnut and orange.

NUTTY ORANGE CHOCOLATE BROWNIES

Preperation time 10 minutes
Cooking time 28 minutes
Makes 14

INGREDIENTS

5 drops vanilla extract
200 grams coconut sugar
55 grams almonds ground
26 grams rice flour
155 grams mixed nuts toasted and chopped
100 grams vegan butter
76 grams plain dark chocolate cacao or use powder
1 orange rind zest

Preperations

Grease tray with vegan butter heat a pan water put bowl on top put chocolate and butter melt until combined, then mix in the other ingredients put mixture in trays in hot oven at 180c for 28 minutes, then remove from oven let coll for 10 minutes then cut into 14 slices, and serve. Even better with home made vegan ice cream.

CHOCO CHUNK & PISACHO SHORTBREAD

Preparation time 10 minutes
Cooking time 18 minutes
Makes 12 slices

INGREDIENTS

55 grams pistachio nuts
100 grams vegan butter
50 grams coconut butter
100 grams corn flour
100 grams rice flour
125 grams dark caco chocolate or powder

Preperations

Use vegan butter to grease tray, get a tray mix vegan butter with the coconut sugar until fluffy, mix in flour chocholate chunks break up 50 grams mix in with pistachio until combined. Put on tray and in oven on 180c for 18 minutes until golden, remove from oven cool for few minutes then cut into 12 slices, plate and serve. Lovely with home made vegan coffee ice cream.

POLENTA & ORANGE COOKIES

Preparation time 10 minutes
Cooking time 8 minutes
Makes 20 cookies

INGREDIENTS

27 grams ground almonds
26 grams rice flour
76 grams polenta
½ tsp baking powder
52 grams vegan butter cut up squares
1 grated orange rind
26 grams almond flakes
50 grams coconut suger or use agave syrup
1 tablespoon flack seed &
3 tablespoons distilled water mixed (instead egg)

Preparation

Get baking tray line with baking paper, get a blender and put in flour, polenta, baking powder, ground almonds, vegan butter, sugar and mix till bread crumb consistency, then add the flack seed mix, orange rind, to form a dough, put in film and fridge for 30 minutes. Get board and flour get dough out dust roll thin to 5mm thick, then cut out 20 cookies put on tray and in oven on 180c for 8 minutes, remove from oven let cool for 3 minutes then serve. You can add dried coconut.

HAZELNUT & CHOCOLATE
CHUNK COOKIES

Preperation time 10 minutes
Cooking time 10 minutes
Makes 28

INGREDIENTS

150 grams hazel nuts
100 grams coconut sugar
76 grams vegan butter
6 tablespoons agave necture
155 grams brown rice flour
1 tablespoon cacao powder
½ tsp bicarbonate soda
80 grams dark cacao choclate
1 tablespoon flack seed &
3 tablespoon of distilled water mixed (instead egg)

Preparation
Get baking tray line with baking paper, then put all ingedients in blender except the chunks of chocolate you broke up and hazel nuts, and blend till a dough, mix in nuts and chunks. Put on board dust and separate into 28 balls, then flatten balls put on tray and in oven on 180c for ten minutes, remove from oven and cool for 3 minutes and serve.

ACCOMPANIMENTS
SIDE DISHES

LIME RELISH CHILLI STRIPS

Preparation time ten minutes
Cooking time ten minutes

INGREDIENTS

½ tsp oregano leave
4 limes
¼ tsp sea salt ground
10 fresh green chillies
½ onion

Preparation

Put chillies in griddle pan and char the skin
turning on all sides then put in oven and bake
on 160c for 15 minutes take out when ready put
aside.

Get board slice onions put in bowl with lime juice, mix in oregano leaves.

Now take chillies and remove skin and seeds then cut chillies in strips adding them to the onion mixture, season with salt. Then cover bowl with film put in fridge for a day to allow lime juice to cook onion and chilli, then serve as a side dish, vegan burger fillings.

GUACAMOLE

Preparation time 10 minutes
Serves 6

INGREDIENTS

3 fresh chillies chopped
¼ tsp sea salt ground
¼ cup chopped coriander
½ onion chopped
2 garlic cloves chopped
4 ripe avocado
1 juice of lime
4 tomatoes

Preparation

Get tomatoes cut cross on them put in bowl of hot water covered for 35 seconds then use scoop to put in bowl cold water drain and peel skins of and remove seeds cut up put aside, chop up all other ingredients and the avocado put in blender and mix, scoop ou put in bowl cover with film and put in fridge for 1 hour before serving.

MANGO CHILLI SALSA

Preparation time ten minutes
Serves 4

INGREDIENTS

1 lime juice and rind
½ white onion
2 ripe mangos
2 fresh red chillies
¼ cup fresh coriander leaves

Preparation

Get board cut chillies deseed slice up then cut
and slice onion, cut mango into cubes then
squeeze juice from line and collect rind also cut
coriander leaves, put all ingredients in bowl and
mix then serve.

CHILLI TOMATO SALSA

Preparation time 10 minutes
Cooking time 40 minutes

INGREDIENTS

2 serrano chillies
1 onion
1 lime juice
520 grams tomatoes
¼ tsp sea salt
½ cup chopped coriander

Preparation

Put oven on 200c get oven dish put tomatoes in in quarters and the chillies roast for 40 minutes, the remove tomato skins and chop up. Cut the onion up finely and put in bowl with the diced tomatoes, lime juice, remove skins off chillies and seeds and slice up then mix in bowl. Now add coriander and the sea salt, cover with film put in fridge for one hour then serve.

COCONUT ONION CHILLI CHUTNEY

Preparation time 10 minutes
Cooking time 10 minutes

INGREDIENTS

1 small onion chopped
¼ cup coriander garnish
2 tablespoon peanut oil
200 grams grated coconut
1/8 cup choppcd mint leaves
3 green chillies chopped with seeds
3 tablespoon lime juice
½ tsp coconut sugar
2 tablespoon coconut milk
2 tablespoon gound nuts
1 tsp fennel seeds

Preparation

Get a blender and put in the chillies coconut,
mint, coriander add two tablespoons lime juice

and mix, put in bowl adding sea salt, coconut milk, coconut sugar and lime juice. Now heat oil in pan and fry the fennel seeds until they start crackling, add onions then lower the heat fry till onion is soft, then put in bowl with coconut mixture and let cool then garnish with fresh coriander leave.

VEGAN MUFFINS, TORTILLA WRAPS & BREAD & PANCAKES

CORN TORTILLAS

Preparation time 20 minutes
Cooking time 15 minutes
Additional 30 minutes
TOTAL 1hr 5 minutes
Seving 12 tortillas

INGREDIENTS

1 1/8 cup distilled water
1 ¾ cups masa harina

Preparation

Get bowl mix distilled water and the masa harina until combined get board flour surface then knead unil smooth and pliable.

If it is to dry add water if to sticky add more masa harina, now wrap in film tightly and leave to sit for 25 minutes, put cast iron griddle on a medium heat then separate dough into 12 balls then use rolling pin and flatten the dough balls. Then place in pan and cook for 45 seconds on each side, repeat till all tortilla are cooked.

VEGAN ZUCCHINI BREAD

Preparation time 20 minutes
Cooking time 1hr 10 minutes
Additional 2 hrs
Total 3hrs 30mins

INGREDIENTS

3 cups all purpose flour not wheat
2 tsp cinnamon ground
½ tsp baking powder
1 tsp sea salt
3 tablespoons flax seeds
1 tsp baking soda
2 ½ cups zucchini shredded
2 tsp vanilla extract
1 cup coconut sugar
¾ cup vegetable oil
1 cup unsweetened apple sauce
¼ cup agave necture

Preperations

Put oven on 160c then greese two 10 inch bread
pans, then mix in bowl the flax seeds, salt,
baking soda, flour, cinnamon, baking powder
and arrowroot until blended then leave to side.
Now mix the coconut sugar, agave necture,
apple sauce, vegetable oil, vanilla extract in
bowl till smooth, then fold in the flour mixture
and the shredded zucchini until moist, divide
the batter mixture between the two bread pans
evenly, then put in oven for 65 minutes then
remove rest for ten 12 minutes, then serve.

VEGAN BANANA MUFFINS

Preparation time 15 minutes
Cooking time 30 minutes
Serves 12

INGREDIENTS

2 cups crushed bananas
1 cup canola oil
1 tsp sea salt ground
1 tsp baking soda
1 tsp nutmcg ground
2 tsp baking powder
2 tsp cinnamon ground
½ cup coconut sugar
¼ cup agave necture
3 cups all purpose flour not wheat
1 cup coconut milk

Preparation

Put the oven on at 170c then grease cups on tray then mix in bowl the coconut sugar, agave necture, flour, cinnamon, baking powder, nutmeg, baking soda, sea salt then in separate bowl mix canola oil, coconut milk and bananas until combined then place in cups in tray, then bake for 30 minutes, take out oven let stand for 3 minutes before serving.

VEGAN PUMPKIN SOURDOUGH SPICED BREAD

Preparation time 20 minutes
Cooking time 55 minutes
Additional 35 minutes
Serves 24

INGREDIENTS

4 ½ cups all purpose flour not wheat
1 ¼ tsp sea salt ground
1 ¾ tsp cinnamon ground
1 ¾ sourdough starter discard
1 tsp ginger grounded
1 tsp baking powder
1 tsp baking soda
¾ tsp cloves
1 cup crushed banana
1 can pumpkin pure
2/3 cup canola oil
1 cup coconut sugar
2 tsp vanilla extract
1/3 cup molasses
¾ cup walnuts chopped
¾ cup raisins

Preperations

Put oven on at 175c and grease two 10 inch
bread pans, put the sourdough discard in bowl
let rest till bubbles start to form for 6 minutes.
Now get a bowl put in cloves, ginger, baking
soda, baking powder, sea salt, flour, cinnamon
and combine.

In a separate bowl mix in the crushed banana,
coconut sugar, oil molasses, pumpkin puree,
vanilla extract and mix very well until no
lumps, now stir in the sourdough discard mix
evenly then add the flour mixture and blend to
thick batter add the walnuts and raisins then
spoon into the two bread pans. Put in oven for
60 minutes then remove let cool for 5 minutes
then put on rack for twenty minutes before
slicing and serving.

VEGAN PANCAKES

Preparation time 5 minutes
Cooking time 10 minutes
Serves 3
Makes 9 pancakes

INGREDIENTS

1 tablespoon sesame seed oil
½ tsp sea salt ground
1 ¼ cups water
2 tablespoon coconut sugar
2 tsp baking powder
1 ¼ cups all purpose flour not wheat

Preparation

To start get a bowl and sift the salt, baking
powder, coconut sugar and flour into it, then in
another bowl whisk the oil and water together
then mix all together well blending with no
lumps.

Then get pan heat sesame seed oil on medium heat and use a soup ladle to pour batter in pan, cook until the pancake bubbles and turn over do the other side till golden, and repeat with each pancake mixture, then serve on plate, with many options of fillings from fresh fruits, lemon honey, maple syrup, cacao and banana and agave necture.

I wish you well on your path to a better diet, a more balanced diet and with plant foods and medicines that are in vibrational tune to the sacred geometric structures, the dodecahedrons and tetrahedrons that build the building blocks the cells of the scaffolding of life, allowing your avatar body to regenerate on a continuum.

I wish you well on your journey to raising your bodies vibration and that of your consciousness, allowing access to your light body and able to ascend, transend and return home in the stars and beyond in the eternal realm of the kingdom of light. NAMASTE LOVELIFELEE

OTHER BOOKS BY LOVELIFELEE

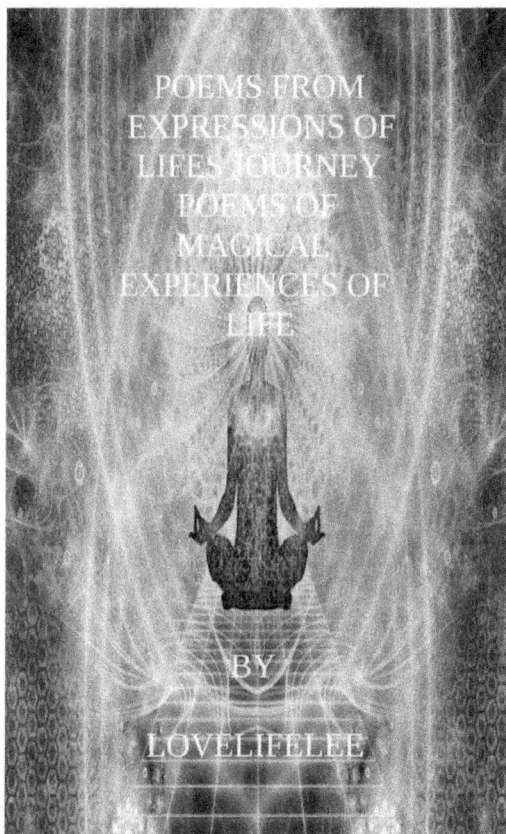

POEMS FROM
EXPRESSIONS OF
LIFES JOURNEY
POEMS OF
MAGICAL
EXPERIENCES OF
LIFE

BY

LOVELIFELEE

FRONT COVER

Expressions of life's journey, poems of mystical experiences on my life's path on planet Gaia & beyond.
Experiences of travelling around the world and off world in the hyper-dimensional matrix, some from in this universe & other eternal realms. Experiences from meditations, ancient spiritual practices, plant medicines of Ayahuasca, Magic Mushrooms, Salvia Divinorum, and different forms of DMT Dimethyltryptamine leaving my body instantly travelling down wormholes entering different dimensions of reality of this holographical light university & realities of the true nature outside time & space in the eternal realm, poems of your immortal light body & the hyper-dimensional matrix the whole of the brahman the creation Namaste lovelifelee

MER-KA-BA

BACK COVER

154

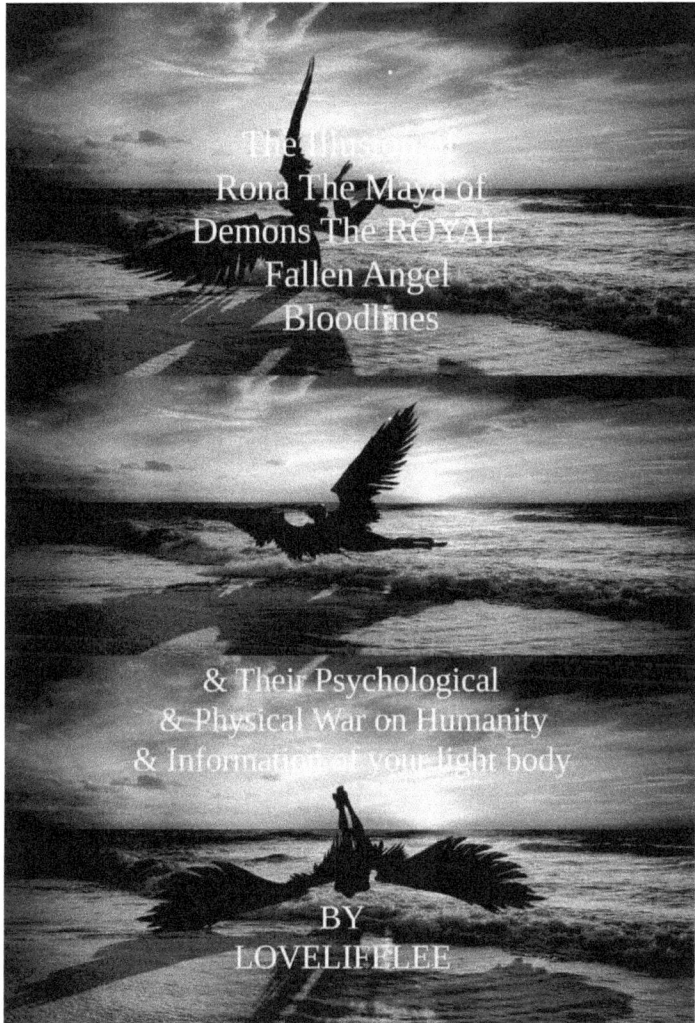

The Illusion of
Rona The Maya of
Demons The ROYAL
Fallen Angel
Bloodlines

& Their Psychological
& Physical War on Humanity
& Information of your light body

BY
LOVELIFELEE

FRONT COVER

MER -KA -BA

(Human)   (Light)   (Body)

Is: This is an explosive, revealing book of ancient knowledge of the blueprint & schematics in your DNA to grow your eternal light body to ascend transcend in the higher dimensional matrix & receive ancient knowledge from the fallen angels governing the royal bloodline/secret orders of satanic cult blood sacrifice/their agendas/cloning/Roman matrix warrior grade microwave weapons, biological weapon vaccines that will rewrite the code of your DNA, then the elite can entrap you to slave your eternal consciousness imprisoned, harvested & written & jinn demonic spirit attachments of the fallen angels.

BACK COVER

OTHER BOOKS BY LOVELIFELEE

156

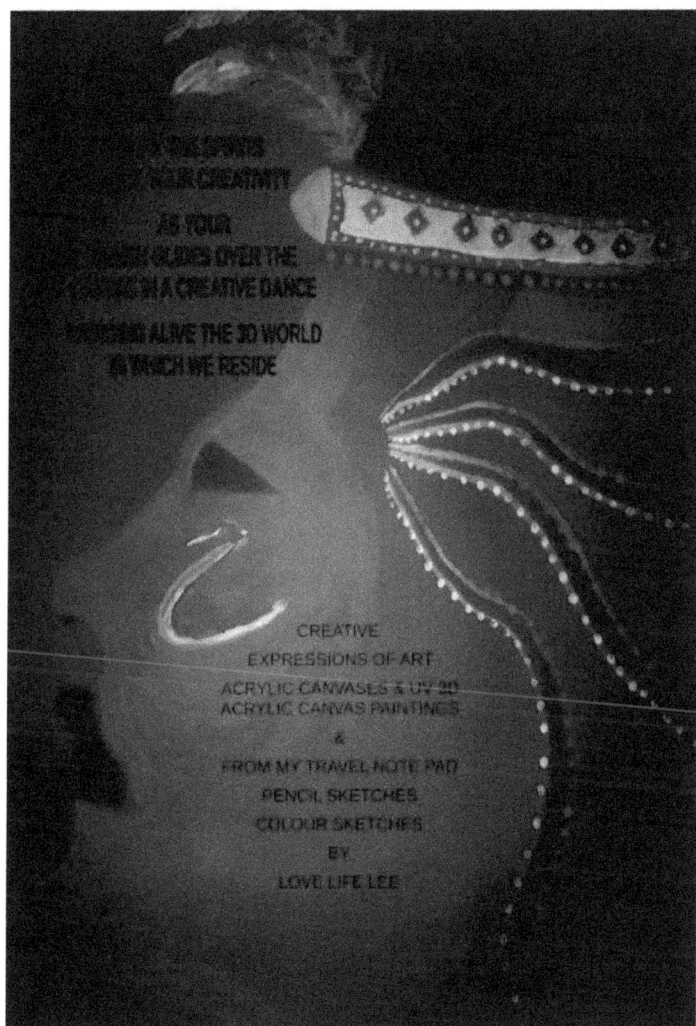

FRONT COVER

EXPRESSIONS FROM WITHIN
CREATIVITY BURSTS FOURTH
THE PENCIL ON MY TRAVEL NOTE PAD
DOODLES & SKETCHES COME ALIVE
SOME WITH COLOUR
THEN THE CANVAS & ACRYLIC PAINTS
CATCH MY EYE
THE BRUSH IN MOTION A NEW WAY
OF EXPRESSION COMES ALIVE
AFTER PRACTICE LUMINOUS UV PAINTS
ADDED MORE ALIVE THEY BE
LAYERING TO CREATE A 3D EFFECT
WITH GLASSES OUT OF THE PAINTING THEY COME
THE ENERGY AND EFFORT CAN BE SEEN
IN THE ART ALIVE WITH SPIRIT
3 DIMENSIONAL ART EXPRESSIONS THEY ARE
DOODLES SKETCHES AND CANVASES
I'VE DRAWN & PAINTED
A SIMPLE ART BOOK TO INSPIRE OTHERS
TO EXPRESS THERE CREATIVITY THROUGH ART
BY LOVE LIFE LEE

BACK COVER

INDEX LIST PAGE